Magical

Diary

With

Spell

Templates

Created by M&M Publications.

Printed by Createspace, an Amazon.com
company.

ISBN-13: 978-1522984504
ISBN-10: 152298450X

Dear Diary,

_____

_____

_____

_____

_____

_____

_____

_____

_____

_____

_____

_____

_____

_____

_____

_____

_____

_____

_____

_____

Date: **Signature:**

____/____/20____   _____

Dear Diary,

_____

_____

_____

_____

_____

_____

_____

_____

_____

_____

_____

_____

_____

_____

_____

_____

_____

_____

_____

Date: **Signature:**

_____/_____/20_____   _____

Dear Diary,

_____

_____

_____

_____

_____

_____

_____

_____

_____

_____

_____

_____

_____

_____

_____

_____

_____

Date: **Signature:**

_____/_____/20_____   _____

Dear Diary,

_____

_____

_____

_____

_____

_____

_____

_____

_____

_____

_____

_____

_____

_____

_____

_____

_____

_____

_____

Date: **Signature:**

_____/_____/20_____   _____

Dear Diary,

_____

_____

_____

_____

_____

_____

_____

_____

_____

_____

_____

_____

_____

_____

_____

_____

_____

_____

_____

Date: **Signature:**

_____/_____/20_____   _____

Dear Diary,

_____

_____

_____

_____

_____

_____

_____

_____

_____

_____

_____

_____

_____

_____

_____

_____

_____

_____

Date: **Signature:**

_____/_____/20_____   _____

Dear Diary,

_____

_____

_____

_____

_____

_____

_____

_____

_____

_____

_____

_____

_____

_____

_____

_____

_____

_____

_____

Date: **Signature:**

_____/_____/20_____   _____

Dear Diary,

_____

_____

_____

_____

_____

_____

_____

_____

_____

_____

_____

_____

_____

_____

_____

_____

_____

_____

_____

_____

Date: **Signature:**

____/____/20____   _____

Dear Diary,

_____

_____

_____

_____

_____

_____

_____

_____

_____

_____

_____

_____

_____

_____

_____

_____

_____

_____

_____

Date: **Signature:**

_____/_____/20____   _____

Dear Diary,

_____

_____

_____

_____

_____

_____

_____

_____

_____

_____

_____

_____

_____

_____

_____

_____

_____

_____

_____

Date: **Signature:**

_____/_____/20_____   _____

Dear Diary,

_____

_____

_____

_____

_____

_____

_____

_____

_____

_____

_____

_____

_____

_____

_____

_____

_____

_____

_____

_____

Date: **Signature:**

_____/_____/20_____   _____

Dear Diary,

_____

_____

_____

_____

_____

_____

_____

_____

_____

_____

_____

_____

_____

_____

_____

_____

_____

_____

_____

Date: **Signature:**

____/____/20____   _____

Dear Diary,

_____

_____

_____

_____

_____

_____

_____

_____

_____

_____

_____

_____

_____

_____

_____

_____

_____

_____

Date: **Signature:**

____/____/20____   _____

Dear Diary,

_____

_____

_____

_____

_____

_____

_____

_____

_____

_____

_____

_____

_____

_____

_____

_____

_____

_____

_____

_____

Date: **Signature:**

_____/_____/20_____   _____

Dear Diary,

_____

_____

_____

_____

_____

_____

_____

_____

_____

_____

_____

_____

_____

_____

_____

_____

_____

_____

Date: **Signature:**

_____/_____/20_____   _____

Dear Diary,

_____

_____

_____

_____

_____

_____

_____

_____

_____

_____

_____

_____

_____

_____

_____

_____

_____

_____

Date: **Signature:**

_____/_____/20____   _____

Dear Diary,

_____

_____

_____

_____

_____

_____

_____

_____

_____

_____

_____

_____

_____

_____

_____

_____

_____

_____

Date: **Signature:**

_____/_____/20____   _____

Dear Diary,

_____

_____

_____

_____

_____

_____

_____

_____

_____

_____

_____

_____

_____

_____

_____

_____

_____

_____

_____

_____

Date: **Signature:**

_____/_____/20_____   _____

Dear Diary,

_____

_____

_____

_____

_____

_____

_____

_____

_____

_____

_____

_____

_____

_____

_____

_____

_____

_____

_____

Date: **Signature:**

_____/_____/20_____   _____

Dear Diary,

_____

_____

_____

_____

_____

_____

_____

_____

_____

_____

_____

_____

_____

_____

_____

_____

_____

_____

_____

Date: **Signature:**

_____/_____/20_____   _____

Dear Diary,

_____

_____

_____

_____

_____

_____

_____

_____

_____

_____

_____

_____

_____

_____

_____

_____

_____

_____

_____

Date: **Signature:**

_____/_____/20_____   _____

Dear Diary,

_____

_____

_____

_____

_____

_____

_____

_____

_____

_____

_____

_____

_____

_____

_____

_____

_____

_____

_____

Date: **Signature:**

_____/_____/20____   _____

Dear Diary,

_____

_____

_____

_____

_____

_____

_____

_____

_____

_____

_____

_____

_____

_____

_____

_____

_____

_____

_____

Date: **Signature:**

_____/_____/20_____   _____

Dear Diary,

_____

_____

_____

_____

_____

_____

_____

_____

_____

_____

_____

_____

_____

_____

_____

_____

_____

_____

Date: **Signature:**

_____/_____/20____   _____

Dear Diary,

_____

_____

_____

_____

_____

_____

_____

_____

_____

_____

_____

_____

_____

_____

_____

_____

_____

_____

_____

_____

Date: **Signature:**

_____/_____/20____   _____

Dear Diary,

_____

_____

_____

_____

_____

_____

_____

_____

_____

_____

_____

_____

_____

_____

_____

_____

_____

_____

_____

Date: **Signature:**

_____/_____/20____   _____

Dear Diary,

_____

_____

_____

_____

_____

_____

_____

_____

_____

_____

_____

_____

_____

_____

_____

_____

_____

_____

Date: **Signature:**

_____/_____/20_____   _____

Dear Diary,

_____

_____

_____

_____

_____

_____

_____

_____

_____

_____

_____

_____

_____

_____

_____

_____

_____

_____

_____

Date: **Signature:**

_____/_____/20____   _____

Dear Diary,

_____

_____

_____

_____

_____

_____

_____

_____

_____

_____

_____

_____

_____

_____

_____

_____

_____

_____

Date: **Signature:**

_____/_____/20_____   _____

Dear Diary,

_____

_____

_____

_____

_____

_____

_____

_____

_____

_____

_____

_____

_____

_____

_____

_____

_____

_____

Date: **Signature:**

_____/_____/20_____   _____

Dear Diary,

_____

_____

_____

_____

_____

_____

_____

_____

_____

_____

_____

_____

_____

_____

_____

_____

_____

_____

Date: **Signature:**

_____/_____/20____   _____

Dear Diary,

_____

_____

_____

_____

_____

_____

_____

_____

_____

_____

_____

_____

_____

_____

_____

_____

_____

_____

_____

_____

Date: **Signature:**

____/____/20____   _____

Dear Diary,

_____

_____

_____

_____

_____

_____

_____

_____

_____

_____

_____

_____

_____

_____

_____

_____

_____

_____

Date: **Signature:**

_____/_____/20_____   _____

Dear Diary,

_____

_____

_____

_____

_____

_____

_____

_____

_____

_____

_____

_____

_____

_____

_____

_____

_____

_____

_____

_____

Date: **Signature:**

_____/_____/20____   _____

Dear Diary,

_____

_____

_____

_____

_____

_____

_____

_____

_____

_____

_____

_____

_____

_____

_____

_____

_____

_____

Date: **Signature:**

_____/_____/20_____   _____

Dear Diary,

_____

_____

_____

_____

_____

_____

_____

_____

_____

_____

_____

_____

_____

_____

_____

_____

_____

_____

Date: **Signature:**

_____/_____/20_____   _____

Dear Diary,

_____

_____

_____

_____

_____

_____

_____

_____

_____

_____

_____

_____

_____

_____

_____

_____

_____

_____

_____

Date: **Signature:**

_____/_____/20_____   _____

Dear Diary,

_____

_____

_____

_____

_____

_____

_____

_____

_____

_____

_____

_____

_____

_____

_____

_____

_____

_____

_____

Date: **Signature:**

_____/_____/20_____   _____

Dear Diary,

_____

_____

_____

_____

_____

_____

_____

_____

_____

_____

_____

_____

_____

_____

_____

_____

_____

_____

Date: **Signature:**

_____/_____/20____   _____

Dear Diary,

_____

_____

_____

_____

_____

_____

_____

_____

_____

_____

_____

_____

_____

_____

_____

_____

_____

_____

Date: **Signature:**

_____/_____/20_____   _____

Dear Diary,

_____

_____

_____

_____

_____

_____

_____

_____

_____

_____

_____

_____

_____

_____

_____

_____

_____

_____

Date: **Signature:**

_____/_____/20_____   _____

Dear Diary,

_____

_____

_____

_____

_____

_____

_____

_____

_____

_____

_____

_____

_____

_____

_____

_____

_____

_____

Date: **Signature:**

_____/_____/20_____   _____

Dear Diary,

_____

_____

_____

_____

_____

_____

_____

_____

_____

_____

_____

_____

_____

_____

_____

_____

_____

_____

_____

Date: **Signature:**

_____/_____/20_____   _____

Dear Diary,

_____

_____

_____

_____

_____

_____

_____

_____

_____

_____

_____

_____

_____

_____

_____

_____

_____

_____

_____

Date: **Signature:**

_____/_____/20____   _____

Dear Diary,

_____

_____

_____

_____

_____

_____

_____

_____

_____

_____

_____

_____

_____

_____

_____

_____

_____

_____

Date: **Signature:**

_____/_____/20_____   _____

Dear Diary,

_____

_____

_____

_____

_____

_____

_____

_____

_____

_____

_____

_____

_____

_____

_____

_____

_____

_____

Date: **Signature:**

_____/_____/20_____   _____

Dear Diary,

_____

_____

_____

_____

_____

_____

_____

_____

_____

_____

_____

_____

_____

_____

_____

_____

_____

_____

Date: **Signature:**

_____/_____/20_____   _____

Dear Diary,

_____

_____

_____

_____

_____

_____

_____

_____

_____

_____

_____

_____

_____

_____

_____

_____

_____

_____

_____

_____

Date: **Signature:**

_____/_____/20_____   _____

Dear Diary,

_____

_____

_____

_____

_____

_____

_____

_____

_____

_____

_____

_____

_____

_____

_____

_____

_____

_____

_____

Date: **Signature:**

_____/_____/20____   _____

Dear Diary,

_____

_____

_____

_____

_____

_____

_____

_____

_____

_____

_____

_____

_____

_____

_____

_____

_____

_____

Date: **Signature:**

_____/_____/20_____   _____

Dear Diary,

_____

_____

_____

_____

_____

_____

_____

_____

_____

_____

_____

_____

_____

_____

_____

_____

_____

Date: **Signature:**

_____/_____/20____   _____

Dear Diary,

_____

_____

_____

_____

_____

_____

_____

_____

_____

_____

_____

_____

_____

_____

_____

_____

_____

_____

_____

Date: **Signature:**

_____/_____/20_____   _____

Dear Diary,

_____

_____

_____

_____

_____

_____

_____

_____

_____

_____

_____

_____

_____

_____

_____

_____

_____

_____

_____

Date: **Signature:**

_____/_____/20_____   _____

Dear Diary,

_____

_____

_____

_____

_____

_____

_____

_____

_____

_____

_____

_____

_____

_____

_____

_____

_____

_____

_____

Date: **Signature:**

_____/_____/20____   _____

Dear Diary,

_____

_____

_____

_____

_____

_____

_____

_____

_____

_____

_____

_____

_____

_____

_____

_____

_____

Date: **Signature:**

_____/_____/20_____   _____

Dear Diary,

_____

_____

_____

_____

_____

_____

_____

_____

_____

_____

_____

_____

_____

_____

_____

_____

_____

_____

Date: **Signature:**

_____/_____/20_____   _____

Dear Diary,

_____

_____

_____

_____

_____

_____

_____

_____

_____

_____

_____

_____

_____

_____

_____

_____

_____

_____

_____

Date: **Signature:**

_____/_____/20____   _____

Dear Diary,

_____

_____

_____

_____

_____

_____

_____

_____

_____

_____

_____

_____

_____

_____

_____

_____

_____

_____

_____

Date: **Signature:**

_____/_____/20____   _____

Dear Diary,

_____

_____

_____

_____

_____

_____

_____

_____

_____

_____

_____

_____

_____

_____

_____

_____

_____

_____

_____

Date: **Signature:**

_____/_____/20____   _____

Dear Diary,

_____

_____

_____

_____

_____

_____

_____

_____

_____

_____

_____

_____

_____

_____

_____

_____

_____

_____

Date: **Signature:**

____/____/20____   _____

Dear Diary,

_____

_____

_____

_____

_____

_____

_____

_____

_____

_____

_____

_____

_____

_____

_____

_____

_____

_____

Date: **Signature:**

_____/_____/20_____   _____

Dear Diary,

_____

_____

_____

_____

_____

_____

_____

_____

_____

_____

_____

_____

_____

_____

_____

_____

_____

_____

Date: **Signature:**

_____/_____/20____   _____

Dear Diary,

_____

_____

_____

_____

_____

_____

_____

_____

_____

_____

_____

_____

_____

_____

_____

_____

_____

_____

Date: **Signature:**

_____/_____/20_____   _____

Dear Diary,

_____

_____

_____

_____

_____

_____

_____

_____

_____

_____

_____

_____

_____

_____

_____

_____

_____

_____

Date: **Signature:**

_____/_____/20____   _____

Dear Diary,

_____

_____

_____

_____

_____

_____

_____

_____

_____

_____

_____

_____

_____

_____

_____

_____

_____

_____

_____

Date: **Signature:**

_____/_____/20_____   _____

Dear Diary,

_____

_____

_____

_____

_____

_____

_____

_____

_____

_____

_____

_____

_____

_____

_____

_____

_____

_____

Date: **Signature:**

_____/_____/20____   _____

Dear Diary,

_____

_____

_____

_____

_____

_____

_____

_____

_____

_____

_____

_____

_____

_____

_____

_____

_____

_____

Date: **Signature:**

_____/_____/20_____   _____

Dear Diary,

_____

_____

_____

_____

_____

_____

_____

_____

_____

_____

_____

_____

_____

_____

_____

_____

_____

_____

Date: **Signature:**

_____/_____/20_____   _____

Dear Diary,

_____

_____

_____

_____

_____

_____

_____

_____

_____

_____

_____

_____

_____

_____

_____

_____

_____

_____

Date: **Signature:**

_____/_____/20_____   _____

Dear Diary,

_____

_____

_____

_____

_____

_____

_____

_____

_____

_____

_____

_____

_____

_____

_____

_____

_____

_____

_____

Date: **Signature:**

_____/_____/20_____   _____

Dear Diary,

_____

_____

_____

_____

_____

_____

_____

_____

_____

_____

_____

_____

_____

_____

_____

_____

_____

_____

Date: **Signature:**

____/____/20____   _____

Dear Diary,

_____

_____

_____

_____

_____

_____

_____

_____

_____

_____

_____

_____

_____

_____

_____

_____

_____

_____

_____

Date: **Signature:**

_____/_____/20_____   _____

Dear Diary,

_____

_____

_____

_____

_____

_____

_____

_____

_____

_____

_____

_____

_____

_____

_____

_____

_____

_____

Date: **Signature:**

_____/_____/20_____   _____

Dear Diary,

_____

_____

_____

_____

_____

_____

_____

_____

_____

_____

_____

_____

_____

_____

_____

_____

_____

_____

Date: **Signature:**

____/____/20____   _____

Dear Diary,

_____

_____

_____

_____

_____

_____

_____

_____

_____

_____

_____

_____

_____

_____

_____

_____

_____

_____

Date: **Signature:**

____/____/20____   _____

Dear Diary,

_____

_____

_____

_____

_____

_____

_____

_____

_____

_____

_____

_____

_____

_____

_____

_____

_____

Date: **Signature:**

_____/_____/20_____   _____

Dear Diary,

_____

_____

_____

_____

_____

_____

_____

_____

_____

_____

_____

_____

_____

_____

_____

_____

_____

_____

Date: **Signature:**

_____/_____/20_____   _____

Dear Diary,

_____

_____

_____

_____

_____

_____

_____

_____

_____

_____

_____

_____

_____

_____

_____

_____

_____

_____

_____

Date: **Signature:**

_____/_____/20____   _____

Dear Diary,

_____

_____

_____

_____

_____

_____

_____

_____

_____

_____

_____

_____

_____

_____

_____

_____

_____

_____

Date: **Signature:**

_____/_____/20____   _____

Dear Diary,

_____

_____

_____

_____

_____

_____

_____

_____

_____

_____

_____

_____

_____

_____

_____

_____

_____

_____

Date: **Signature:**

_____/_____/20_____   _____

Dear Diary,

_____

_____

_____

_____

_____

_____

_____

_____

_____

_____

_____

_____

_____

_____

_____

_____

_____

_____

Date: **Signature:**

_____/_____/20_____   _____

Dear Diary,

_____

_____

_____

_____

_____

_____

_____

_____

_____

_____

_____

_____

_____

_____

_____

_____

_____

_____

_____

Date: **Signature:**

_____/_____/20____   _____

Dear Diary,

_____

_____

_____

_____

_____

_____

_____

_____

_____

_____

_____

_____

_____

_____

_____

_____

_____

_____

Date: **Signature:**

_____/_____/20_____   _____

Dear Diary,

_____

_____

_____

_____

_____

_____

_____

_____

_____

_____

_____

_____

_____

_____

_____

_____

_____

_____

_____

Date: **Signature:**

_____/_____/**20**____   _____

Dear Diary,

_____

_____

_____

_____

_____

_____

_____

_____

_____

_____

_____

_____

_____

_____

_____

_____

_____

_____

_____

Date: **Signature:**

_____/_____/20_____   _____

Dear Diary,

_____

_____

_____

_____

_____

_____

_____

_____

_____

_____

_____

_____

_____

_____

_____

_____

_____

_____

_____

Date: **Signature:**

_____/_____/20_____   _____

Dear Diary,

_____

_____

_____

_____

_____

_____

_____

_____

_____

_____

_____

_____

_____

_____

_____

_____

_____

_____

Date: **Signature:**

____/____/20____   _____

Dear Diary,

_____

_____

_____

_____

_____

_____

_____

_____

_____

_____

_____

_____

_____

_____

_____

_____

_____

_____

Date: **Signature:**

_____/_____/20_____   _____

Dear Diary,

_____

_____

_____

_____

_____

_____

_____

_____

_____

_____

_____

_____

_____

_____

_____

_____

_____

_____

_____

Date: **Signature:**

_____/_____/20_____   _____

Dear Diary,

_____

_____

_____

_____

_____

_____

_____

_____

_____

_____

_____

_____

_____

_____

_____

_____

_____

_____

_____

Date: **Signature:**

_____/_____/20_____   _____

Dear Diary,

_____

_____

_____

_____

_____

_____

_____

_____

_____

_____

_____

_____

_____

_____

_____

_____

_____

_____

_____

Date: **Signature:**

_____/_____/20____   _____

Dear Diary,

_____

_____

_____

_____

_____

_____

_____

_____

_____

_____

_____

_____

_____

_____

_____

_____

_____

_____

_____

Date: **Signature:**

_____/_____/20_____   _____

Dear Diary,

_____

_____

_____

_____

_____

_____

_____

_____

_____

_____

_____

_____

_____

_____

_____

_____

_____

_____

_____

Date: **Signature:**

_____/_____/20____   _____

Dear Diary,

_____

_____

_____

_____

_____

_____

_____

_____

_____

_____

_____

_____

_____

_____

_____

_____

_____

_____

Date: **Signature:**

_____/_____/20_____   _____

Dear Diary,

_____

_____

_____

_____

_____

_____

_____

_____

_____

_____

_____

_____

_____

_____

_____

_____

_____

_____

_____

Date: **Signature:**

____/____/20____   _____

Dear Diary,

_____

_____

_____

_____

_____

_____

_____

_____

_____

_____

_____

_____

_____

_____

_____

_____

_____

_____

Date: **Signature:**

_____/_____/20____   _____

Dear Diary,

_____

_____

_____

_____

_____

_____

_____

_____

_____

_____

_____

_____

_____

_____

_____

_____

_____

_____

Date: **Signature:**

_____/_____/20_____   _____

Dear Diary,

_____

_____

_____

_____

_____

_____

_____

_____

_____

_____

_____

_____

_____

_____

_____

_____

_____

_____

_____

_____

Date: **Signature:**

_____/_____/20_____   _____

Dear Diary,

_____

_____

_____

_____

_____

_____

_____

_____

_____

_____

_____

_____

_____

_____

_____

_____

_____

_____

Date: **Signature:**

____/____/20____   _____

Dear Diary,

_____

_____

_____

_____

_____

_____

_____

_____

_____

_____

_____

_____

_____

_____

_____

_____

_____

_____

_____

Date: **Signature:**

_____/_____/20_____   _____

Dear Diary,

_____

_____

_____

_____

_____

_____

_____

_____

_____

_____

_____

_____

_____

_____

_____

_____

_____

_____

Date: **Signature:**

_____/_____/20_____   _____

Dear Diary,

_____

_____

_____

_____

_____

_____

_____

_____

_____

_____

_____

_____

_____

_____

_____

_____

_____

_____

_____

Date: **Signature:**

_____/_____/20_____   _____

Dear Diary,

_____

_____

_____

_____

_____

_____

_____

_____

_____

_____

_____

_____

_____

_____

_____

_____

_____

_____

Date: **Signature:**

____/____/20____   _____

Dear Diary,

_____

_____

_____

_____

_____

_____

_____

_____

_____

_____

_____

_____

_____

_____

_____

_____

_____

_____

_____

Date: **Signature:**

_____/_____/20_____   _____

Dear Diary,

_____

_____

_____

_____

_____

_____

_____

_____

_____

_____

_____

_____

_____

_____

_____

_____

_____

_____

_____

Date: **Signature:**

_____/_____/20_____   _____

Dear Diary,

_____

_____

_____

_____

_____

_____

_____

_____

_____

_____

_____

_____

_____

_____

_____

_____

_____

_____

_____

Date: **Signature:**

_____/_____/20_____   _____

Dear Diary,

_____

_____

_____

_____

_____

_____

_____

_____

_____

_____

_____

_____

_____

_____

_____

_____

_____

_____

_____

Date: **Signature:**

____/____/20____   _____

Dear Diary,

_____

_____

_____

_____

_____

_____

_____

_____

_____

_____

_____

_____

_____

_____

_____

_____

_____

_____

_____

Date: **Signature:**

____/____/20____   _____

Dear Diary,

_____

_____

_____

_____

_____

_____

_____

_____

_____

_____

_____

_____

_____

_____

_____

_____

_____

_____

_____

Date: **Signature:**

_____/_____/20____   _____

Dear Diary,

_____

_____

_____

_____

_____

_____

_____

_____

_____

_____

_____

_____

_____

_____

_____

_____

_____

_____

_____

Date: **Signature:**

_____/_____/20____   _____

Dear Diary,

_____

_____

_____

_____

_____

_____

_____

_____

_____

_____

_____

_____

_____

_____

_____

_____

_____

_____

Date: **Signature:**

_____/_____/20_____   _____

Dear Diary,

_____

_____

_____

_____

_____

_____

_____

_____

_____

_____

_____

_____

_____

_____

_____

_____

_____

_____

Date: **Signature:**

_____/_____/20_____   _____

Dear Diary,

_____

_____

_____

_____

_____

_____

_____

_____

_____

_____

_____

_____

_____

_____

_____

_____

_____

_____

Date: **Signature:**

_____/_____/20_____   _____

Dear Diary,

_____

_____

_____

_____

_____

_____

_____

_____

_____

_____

_____

_____

_____

_____

_____

_____

_____

_____

_____

Date: **Signature:**

_____/_____/20____   _____

Dear Diary,

_____

_____

_____

_____

_____

_____

_____

_____

_____

_____

_____

_____

_____

_____

_____

_____

_____

_____

Date: **Signature:**

_____/_____/20_____   _____

Dear Diary,

_____

_____

_____

_____

_____

_____

_____

_____

_____

_____

_____

_____

_____

_____

_____

_____

_____

_____

_____

_____

Date: **Signature:**

_____/_____/20_____   _____

Dear Diary,

_____

_____

_____

_____

_____

_____

_____

_____

_____

_____

_____

_____

_____

_____

_____

_____

_____

_____

Date: **Signature:**

_____/_____/20____   _____

Dear Diary,

_____

_____

_____

_____

_____

_____

_____

_____

_____

_____

_____

_____

_____

_____

_____

_____

_____

_____

Date: **Signature:**

_____/_____/20____   _____

Dear Diary,

_____

_____

_____

_____

_____

_____

_____

_____

_____

_____

_____

_____

_____

_____

_____

_____

_____

_____

_____

Date: **Signature:**

_____/_____/20_____   _____

Dear Diary,

_____

_____

_____

_____

_____

_____

_____

_____

_____

_____

_____

_____

_____

_____

_____

_____

_____

_____

_____

Date: **Signature:**

_____/_____/20_____   _____

Dear Diary,

_____

_____

_____

_____

_____

_____

_____

_____

_____

_____

_____

_____

_____

_____

_____

_____

_____

Date: **Signature:**

_____/_____/20_____   _____

Spell
Templates

Spell Template #_____

Spell Items:

_____ _____

_____ _____

_____ _____

_____ _____

Moon Phase:

Hour: 6-7-8-9-10-11-12-13-14-15-16-17-18-19-20-21-22-23-24-1-2-3-4-5

Spell Casting: _____

_____

_____

_____

_____

_____

_____

Spell Template #_____

Spell Items:

_____   _____

_____   _____

_____   _____

_____   _____

Moon Phase:

Hour: 6-7-8-9-10-11-12-13-14-15-16-17-18-19-20-21-22-23-24-1-2-3-4-5

Spell Casting: _____

_____

_____

_____

_____

_____

_____

Spell Template #_____

Spell Items:

_____   _____

_____   _____

_____   _____

_____   _____

Moon Phase:

Hour: 6-7-8-9-10-11-12-13-14-15-16-
17-18-19-20-21-22-23-24-1-2-3-4-5

Spell Casting: _____

_____

_____

_____

_____

_____

_____

Spell Template #_____

Spell Items:

_____   _____

_____   _____

_____   _____

_____   _____

Moon Phase:

Hour: 6-7-8-9-10-11-12-13-14-15-16-
17-18-19-20-21-22-23-24-1-2-3-4-5

Spell Casting: _____

_____

_____

_____

_____

_____

_____

Spell Template #_____

Spell Items:

_____   _____

_____   _____

_____   _____

_____   _____

Moon Phase:

Hour: 6-7-8-9-10-11-12-13-14-15-16-17-18-19-20-21-22-23-24-1-2-3-4-5

Spell Casting: _____

_____

_____

_____

_____

_____

_____

Spell Template #_____

Spell Items:

_____   _____

_____   _____

_____   _____

_____   _____

Moon Phase:

Hour: 6-7-8-9-10-11-12-13-14-15-16-17-18-19-20-21-22-23-24-1-2-3-4-5

Spell Casting: _____

_____

_____

_____

_____

_____

_____

Spell Template #_____

Spell Items:

_____ _____

_____ _____

_____ _____

_____ _____

Moon Phase:

Hour: 6-7-8-9-10-11-12-13-14-15-16-17-18-19-20-21-22-23-24-1-2-3-4-5

Spell Casting: _____

_____

_____

_____

_____

_____

_____

Spell Template #_____

Spell Items:

_____   _____

_____   _____

_____   _____

_____   _____

Moon Phase:

Hour: 6-7-8-9-10-11-12-13-14-15-16-
17-18-19-20-21-22-23-24-1-2-3-4-5

Spell Casting: _____

_____

_____

_____

_____

_____

_____

Spell Template #_____

Spell Items:

_____   _____

_____   _____

_____   _____

_____   _____

Moon Phase:

Hour: 6-7-8-9-10-11-12-13-14-15-16-17-18-19-20-21-22-23-24-1-2-3-4-5

Spell Casting: _____

_____

_____

_____

_____

_____

_____

Spell Template #_____

Spell Items:

_____   _____

_____   _____

_____   _____

_____   _____

Moon Phase:

Hour: 6-7-8-9-10-11-12-13-14-15-16-17-18-19-20-21-22-23-24-1-2-3-4-5

Spell Casting: _____

_____

_____

_____

_____

_____

_____

Spell Template #_____

Spell Items:

_____   _____

_____   _____

_____   _____

_____   _____

Moon Phase:

Hour: 6-7-8-9-10-11-12-13-14-15-16-17-18-19-20-21-22-23-24-1-2-3-4-5

Spell Casting: _____

_____

_____

_____

_____

_____

_____

Spell Template #_____

Spell Items:

_____   _____

_____   _____

_____   _____

_____   _____

Moon Phase:

Hour: 6-7-8-9-10-11-12-13-14-15-16-17-18-19-20-21-22-23-24-1-2-3-4-5

Spell Casting: _____

_____

_____

_____

_____

_____

_____

Spell Template #_____

Spell Items:

_____   _____

_____   _____

_____   _____

_____   _____

Moon Phase:

Hour: 6-7-8-9-10-11-12-13-14-15-16-17-18-19-20-21-22-23-24-1-2-3-4-5

Spell Casting: _____

_____

_____

_____

_____

_____

_____

Spell Template #_____

Spell Items:

_____ _____

_____ _____

_____ _____

_____ _____

Moon Phase:

Hour: 6-7-8-9-10-11-12-13-14-15-16-17-18-19-20-21-22-23-24-1-2-3-4-5

Spell Casting: _____

_____

_____

_____

_____

_____

_____

Spell Template #_____

Spell Items:

_____   _____

_____   _____

_____   _____

_____   _____

Moon Phase:

Hour: 6-7-8-9-10-11-12-13-14-15-16-17-18-19-20-21-22-23-24-1-2-3-4-5

Spell Casting: _____

_____

_____

_____

_____

_____

_____

Spell Template #_____

Spell Items:

_____   _____

_____   _____

_____   _____

_____   _____

Moon Phase:

Hour: 6-7-8-9-10-11-12-13-14-15-16-17-18-19-20-21-22-23-24-1-2-3-4-5

Spell Casting: _____

_____

_____

_____

_____

_____

_____

Spell Template #_____

Spell Items:

_____ _____

_____ _____

_____ _____

_____ _____

Moon Phase:

Hour: 6-7-8-9-10-11-12-13-14-15-16-17-18-19-20-21-22-23-24-1-2-3-4-5

Spell Casting: _____

_____

_____

_____

_____

_____

_____

Spell Template #_____

Spell Items:

_____   _____

_____   _____

_____   _____

_____   _____

Moon Phase:

Hour: 6-7-8-9-10-11-12-13-14-15-16-17-18-19-20-21-22-23-24-1-2-3-4-5

Spell Casting: _____

_____

_____

_____

_____

_____

_____

Spell Template #_____

Spell Items:

_____   _____

_____   _____

_____   _____

_____   _____

Moon Phase:

Hour: 6-7-8-9-10-11-12-13-14-15-16-17-18-19-20-21-22-23-24-1-2-3-4-5

Spell Casting: _____

_____

_____

_____

_____

_____

Spell Template #_____

Spell Items:

_____ _____

_____ _____

_____ _____

_____ _____

Moon Phase:

Hour: 6-7-8-9-10-11-12-13-14-15-16-17-18-19-20-21-22-23-24-1-2-3-4-5

Spell Casting: _____

_____

_____

_____

_____

_____

_____

Spell Template #_____

Spell Items:

_____   _____

_____   _____

_____   _____

_____   _____

Moon Phase:

Hour: 6-7-8-9-10-11-12-13-14-15-16-17-18-19-20-21-22-23-24-1-2-3-4-5

Spell Casting: _____

_____

_____

_____

_____

_____

_____

Spell Template #_____

Spell Items:

_____   _____

_____   _____

_____   _____

_____   _____

Moon Phase:

Hour: 6-7-8-9-10-11-12-13-14-15-16-17-18-19-20-21-22-23-24-1-2-3-4-5

Spell Casting: _____

_____

_____

_____

_____

_____

_____

Spell Template #_____

Spell Items:

_____   _____

_____   _____

_____   _____

_____   _____

Moon Phase:

Hour: 6-7-8-9-10-11-12-13-14-15-16-17-18-19-20-21-22-23-24-1-2-3-4-5

Spell Casting: _____

_____

_____

_____

_____

_____

_____

Spell Template #_____

Spell Items:

_____   _____

_____   _____

_____   _____

_____   _____

Moon Phase:

Hour: 6-7-8-9-10-11-12-13-14-15-16-17-18-19-20-21-22-23-24-1-2-3-4-5

Spell Casting: _____

_____

_____

_____

_____

_____

_____

Spell Template #_____

Spell Items:

_____ _____

_____ _____

_____ _____

_____ _____

Moon Phase:

Hour: 6-7-8-9-10-11-12-13-14-15-16-17-18-19-20-21-22-23-24-1-2-3-4-5

Spell Casting: _____

_____

_____

_____

_____

_____

_____

Spell Template #_____

Spell Items:

_____ _____

_____ _____

_____ _____

_____ _____

Moon Phase:

Hour: 6-7-8-9-10-11-12-13-14-15-16-17-18-19-20-21-22-23-24-1-2-3-4-5

Spell Casting: _____

_____

_____

_____

_____

_____

_____

Spell Template #_____

Spell Items:

_____   _____

_____   _____

_____   _____

_____   _____

Moon Phase:

Hour: 6-7-8-9-10-11-12-13-14-15-16-17-18-19-20-21-22-23-24-1-2-3-4-5

Spell Casting: _____

_____

_____

_____

_____

_____

_____

Spell Template #_____

Spell Items:

_____ _____

_____ _____

_____ _____

_____ _____

Moon Phase:

Hour: 6-7-8-9-10-11-12-13-14-15-16-17-18-19-20-21-22-23-24-1-2-3-4-5

Spell Casting: _____

_____

_____

_____

_____

_____

_____